OLYMPUS

OM-D E-M1 Mark III

POCK

TABLE OF CONTENTS

12. Info Button: Use to cycle through information screens.

13. Playback Button: Press to review images on the monitor.

14. ISO Button: Press to open the ISO screen and select an ISO with the Front or Rear dial.

15. Memory Cards Slots (Under Cover on Side): There are two SD/SDHC/SDXC memory card slots.

CAMERA BODY BOTTOM

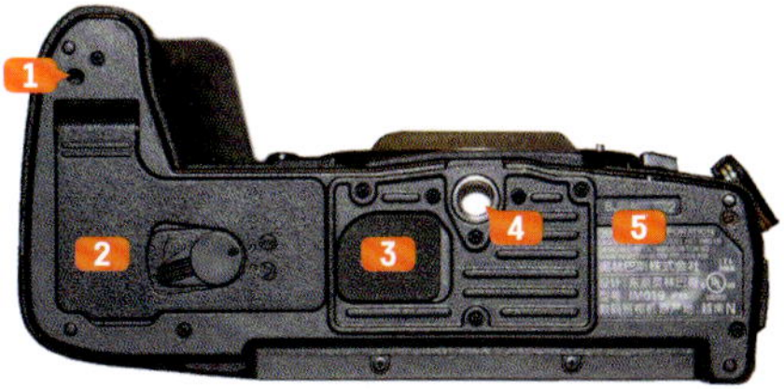

1. Power Battery Holder (PBH) Pin Hole: Use to align and attach an external battery grip.

2. Battery Compartment: Where the camera battery goes.

3. Power Battery Holder Electronic Connectors (Under Rubber Cover): Remove cover if using an external battery grip.

4. Tripod Socket: Use to attach tripod or monopod.

5. Camera ID Plate: Shows camera information and serial number.

CAMERA BODY SIDE

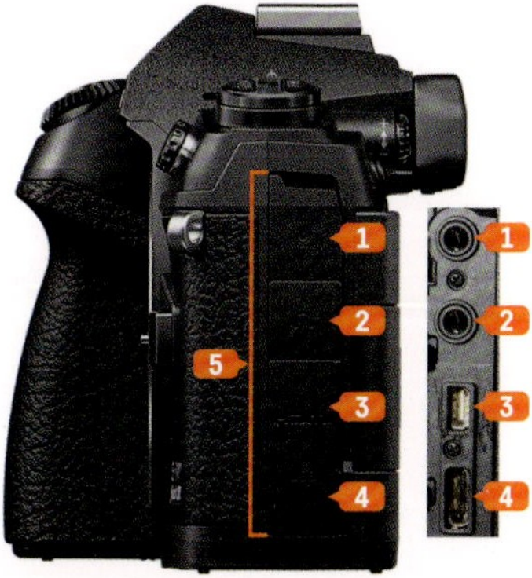

1. **Microphone Connector:** Use to connect external microphone or line-in audio.
2. **Headphone Connector:** Use to connect headphones.
3. **HDMI Connector (Type D):** Use to connect HDMI Micro (type D) cable.
4. **USB Connector (Type C):** Use to connect USB type C cable.
5. **Rubber Cover (Shown Closed):** Rubber cover that protects connectors.

VIEWFINDER / LIVE VIEW SCREEN

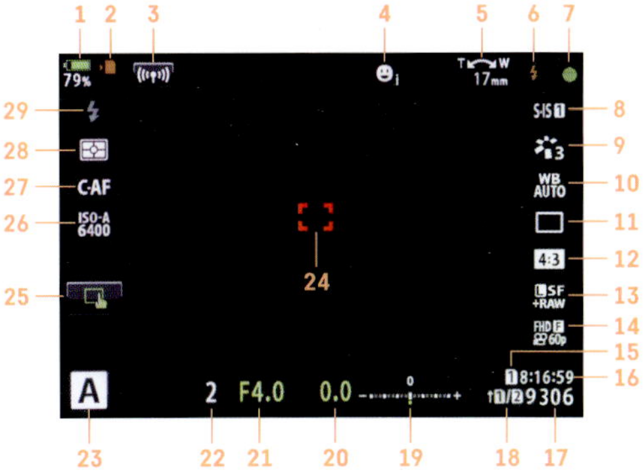

1. Battery Level
2. Card Write Indicator
3. Wi-Fi
4. Face Priority/Eye Priority
5. Lens Focal Length/Zoom Operation Direction
6. Flash Status
7. AF Confirmation Mark
8. Image Stabilizer
9. Picture Mode
10. White Balance
11. Drive Mode
12. Aspect Ratio
13. Image Quality
14. Movie Image Quality
15. Movie Save Slot

16. Movie Recording Time Available
17. Image Capacity for Memory Card
18. Save Settings for Memory Cards
19. Exposure Compensation (Yellow) and Flash Intensity (White) Indicator Scale
20. Numerical Exposure Compensation Value
21. Aperture
22. Shutter Speed
23. Shooting Mode
24. AF Point Indicator
25. Touch Screen Operations Control
26. ISO Mode/Sensitivity
27. AF Mode
28. Metering Mode
29. Flash Mode

SUPER CONTROL PANEL / LIVE VIEW SUPER CONTROL PANEL

The Super Control Panel allows quick access to the following settings. Use the Arrow Key Pad to select the setting, and press OK to open that setting's adjustment options.

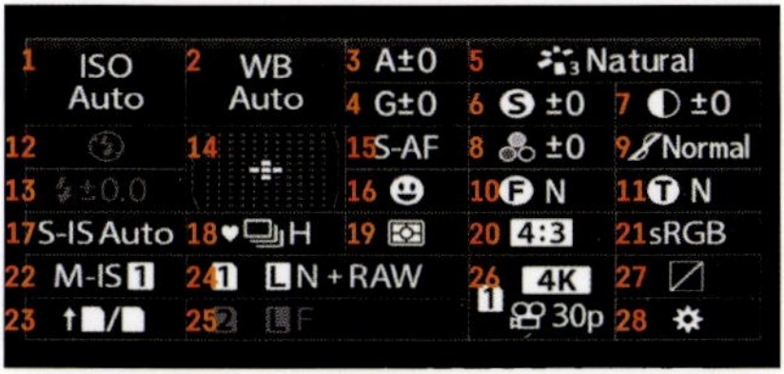

1. ISO Mode/Sensitivity
2. White Balance
3. Amber Tint in White Balance
4. Green Tint in White Balance
5. Picture Mode
6. Sharpness Setting of Picture Mode
7. Contrast Setting of Picture Mode
8. Saturation Setting of Picture Mode
9. Gradation Setting of Picture Mode
10. Color Filter Setting (for Monochrome)
11. Toning Setting (for Monochrome)
12. Flash Mode
13. Manual Value for Flash Mode/Flash Intensity Control
14. Autofocus Area
15. Autofocus Mode
16. Face Priority
17. Image Stabilizer
18. Drive Mode
19. Metering Mode
20. Aspect Ratio
21. Color Space
22. Movie Image Stabilizer
23. Save Settings for Memory Cards
24. Card 1 Image Quality
25. Card 2 Image Quality
26. Movie Image Quality
27. Highlight and Shadow Control
28. Button Function Assignment

03 ESSENTIAL MODES AND SETTINGS

SHOOTING MODES

Press the Mode Dial Lock button down to unlock the Mode dial, then turn the dial to the desired Shooting mode. Press the Mode Dial Lock button a second time to lock in your selection.

P (Program): The camera sets the shutter speed and aperture based on metering info and the current ISO.

A (Aperture Priority): You set the aperture, and the camera sets the shutter speed based on metering info and the current ISO. The range of available apertures depends on the attached lens.

S (Shutter Speed Priority): You set the shutter speed and the camera sets the aperture based on metering info and the current ISO.

M (Manual): You set the ISO, shutter speed, and aperture.

B (Bulb): Use for long exposures. The shutter remains open as long as the Shutter button is pressed.

C1-C4 (Custom Shooting Modes): Use to store custom shooting settings that are easily retrieved.

Movie: Use to record movies.

METERING MODES

Press the AF/Metering Mode button and rotate the Front dial to select a Metering mode.

Digital ESP Metering: The camera divides the scene into 324 areas and tries to determine the best exposure by taking the nature of the scene into consideration. Works well for most scenes, including back-lit subjects.

Center Weighted Averaging Metering: The camera looks at the whole scene but gives more emphasis to the area in the center.

Spot Metering: The camera uses a small area (approximately 2% of the frame) to determine exposure.

Spot Metering (Highlight): The camera uses a small area to determine exposure but works to keep bright subjects appearing bright.

Spot Metering (Shadow): The camera uses a small area to determine exposure but works to keep dark subjects appearing dark.

EXPOSURE COMPENSATION

When using P, A, S, or M Shooting mode, press the Exposure Compensation button and turn the Front or Rear dial to adjust the exposure from –5 to +5 stops.

Note: When using M (Manual) Shooting mode, Auto ISO must be used in order to enable exposure compensation.

FOCUS MODES

Press the AF/Metering Mode button, rotate the Rear dial to select a Focus mode, then press OK.

S-AF (Single AF): The camera focuses once when the Shutter button is pressed halfway down. Best used for static subjects.

C-AF (Continuous AF): The camera starts to focus when the Shutter button is pressed halfway down and continues to focus until the photo is taken.

MF (Manual Focus): Focus is achieved by rotating the focus ring on the lens.

C-AF + TR (Continuous AF + Tracking): The camera starts to focus when the Shutter button is pressed halfway down and will try to track the subject until the photo is taken. This cannot be used with: keystone compensation, High Res Shot, focus stacking, interval timer, HDR, live ND filter, or fisheye correction.

PreMF (Preset Manual Focus): The camera automatically focuses on the preset focus point when shooting.

[*]AF (Starry Sky AF): Use to photograph pictures of stars in the night sky. See Section 4.

AUTOFOCUS TARGET MODES

Press and hold the Multi Selector and rotate the Front or Rear dial to cycle through and choose an AF target mode.

Single Target: The camera uses a single focus target.

Small Target: The smallest available focus target. Use for pinpoint focus on small subjects.

5-Target Group: Uses five focus targets arranged in a cross formation. The camera picks which of the five focus targets to use from the group.

9-Target Group (3 x 3): Uses a group of nine targets arranged in a 3 x 3 square. The camera picks which of the nine focus targets to use.

25-Target Group (5 x 5): Uses a group of 25 targets arranged in a 5 x 5 square. The camera picks which of the 25 focus targets to use.

All Targets: The camera picks which focus target to use from all the targets: 121 targets in an 11 x 11 grid for still photos, and 99 targets in an 11 x 9 grid for movies.

C1–C4 Custom Target: You can create four custom focus target sizes in the Menu > Custom Menu > A2 > Target Mode Settings menu.

DRIVE MODES

Press the Sequential Shooting/Self-Timer/Flash button and rotate the Rear dial to select a Drive mode, then press OK.

Single: The camera takes a single frame each time the Shutter button is pressed all the way down.

Sequential High: The camera takes up to 15 fps (frames per second) while the Shutter button is held down. The focus, exposure, and white balance are locked at the values for the first shot.

Sequential Low: The camera takes up to 10 fps while the Shutter button is held down.

12-Second Self-Timer: The camera takes a photo 12 seconds after the Shutter button is pressed all the way down. The self-timer lamp will illuminate for the first 10 seconds and flash for the last two seconds. The focus is achieved when the Shutter button is pressed halfway down.

2-Second Self-Timer: The camera takes a photo two seconds after the Shutter button is pressed all the way down. The self-timer lamp will flash for the two seconds. The focus is achieved when the Shutter button is pressed halfway down.

Custom Self-Timer: You determine the self-timer delay and the number of shots taken when the timer expires. When selected, press the INFO button before pressing OK to adjust settings.

Anti-Shock: The camera tries to reduce any blurring caused by the shutter motion. Can be used with Single, Sequential Low, and Self-Timer modes. This mode is not on by default and needs to be enabled in the Menu > Custom Menu > D1 > Sequential Shooting/Self-Timer Settings menu.

Silent: The camera uses the electronic shutter for quieter operation. Can be used with Single, Sequential Low, Sequential High, and Self-Timer modes. When using Sequential High, you can have frame rate of up to 60 fps.

Pro Capture High: Allows photos to be taken with no shutter lag and captures up to 60 fps. See Section 4.

Pro Capture Low: Allows photos to be taken with no shutter lag and captures up to 18 fps. See Section 4.

High Res Shot: Allows for high-resolution images to be taken in either Handheld or Tripod mode. See Section 4.

WHITE BALANCE

Press the OK button to open the Super Control Panel, use the Arrow Key Pad to navigate to WB, and use the Front dial to select a white balance setting.

AUTO is the setting best suited for most situations. You can use specific preset white balance settings (Daylight, Shade, Cloudy, etc.) when shooting under specific lighting conditions, or you can create a custom white balance using the One-Touch White Balance feature (see Section 4).

IMAGE SIZE/QUALITY

Press the OK button to open the Super Control Panel, use the Arrow Key Pad to select the Image Quality icon, and use the Front dial to select the desired setting. The available combinations of image sizes and compression rates are set in the Menu > Custom Menu > G > Image Quality [icon] Settings menu.

LSF: 5184 x 3888 SuperFine Compression JPEG

LF: 5184 x 3888 Fine Compression JPEG

LN: 5184 x 3888 Normal Compression JPEG

MN: 3200 x 2400 Normal Compression JPEG

RAW: 5184 x 3888 Lossless Compression ORF

RAW + JPEG: ORF + JPEG

04 OTHER HELPFUL SETTINGS

PICTURE MODES

Press the OK button to open the Super Control Panel, use the Arrow Key Pad to navigate to Picture Mode, and use the Front dial to select the desired setting.

i-Enhance: Camera adjusts the colors and contrast for the best results automatically.

Vivid: Creates a more vivid look.

Natural: Creates natural-looking colors.

Muted: Best for images that will be retouched later.

Portrait: Use for people photos, as it enhances skin tone.

Monochrome: Records images in monochrome. You can add color filters and/or tinting.

Custom: Adjust a Picture mode to create a custom version.

e-Portrait: The camera tries to smooth complexions in portrait photographs.

Underwater: Use to preserve colors captured underwater.

Color Creator: Allows you to adjust the hue and color.

Art Modes: These modes allow for creative presets and filters to be used. Art modes include Pop Art, Soft Focus, Pale & Light Color, Light Tone, Grainy Film, Pin Hole, Diorama, Cross Process, Gentle Sepia, Dramatic Tone, Key Line, Watercolor, Vintage, Partial Color, Bleach Bypass, and Instant Film.

Flat and OM-Log400: Two Picture modes available when shooting movies. Flat uses a tone curve adapted to color grading, and OM-Log400 uses a log tone curve for more flexibility for color grading.

COLOR SPACE

Press the OK button to open the Super Control Panel, use the Arrow Key Pad to navigate to Color Space, and use the Front dial to select the desired setting.

sRGB: Smaller color space. Best when images are used directly from the camera.

Adobe RGB: Larger color space. Best used when images will be edited with software.

ONE-TOUCH WHITE BALANCE

The One-Touch White Balance feature allows you to quickly set a custom white balance by using a white piece of paper (or other white object) in your scene as a white balance reference.

1. Press and hold the One-Touch White Balance button.
2. Aim the camera at a piece of white paper (fill the frame with the paper) and press the Shutter button.
3. Use the Arrow Key Pad to assign the custom white balance to one of the four custom White Balance slots.
4. Press OK.

AUTO ISO

Press the ISO button and rotate the Front or Rear dial to select ISO AUTO.

Go to the Menu > Custom Menu > E1 > ISO-Auto Set menu to determine the maximum ISO sensitivity and lowest Shutter Speed settings.

EXPOSURE BRACKETING

Menu > Shooting Menu 2 > Bracketing

1. Select Bracketing and press OK. Press the Right Arrow key, select On and press the Right Arrow key again.
2. Select AE BKT and press the Right Arrow key.
3. Select the desired Exposure Bracketing settings (e.g., number of shots, bracketing amounts, etc.) from the list, and press OK.
4. Press the Menu button, make sure On is selected, and press OK to save your changes and exit.

Bracketing is now turned on until you return to this menu and turn it off.

Note: The bracketing menu also allows you to bracket the following settings: White Balance, Flash, ISO, Art filter (creates a copy with each of the Art filter settings applied), and Focus. Make sure you turn bracketing off once you're finished.

INFORMATION DISPLAY

Press the Info button while shooting to switch between information screens.

The view will cycle through the following screens: Basic Information > Image Only > Histogram Display (Custom 1) >

Level Gauge Display (Custom 2). The items shown in Custom 1 and 2 are chosen in the Menu > Custom Menu > D1 > Info Settings > LV-Info > Custom 1 (and Custom 2) menus, where you can set the display to Histogram, Highlights & Shadow, or Level Gauge.

PRO CAPTURE

Press the Sequential Shooting/Self-Timer/Flash button, rotate the Rear dial to select Pro Capture High (or Pro Capture Low), and press OK.

The Pro Capture feature allows you to start recording images when the Shutter button is pressed halfway down, resulting in no camera lag when you press the Shutter button all the way down to take photos. Use Pro Capture High to capture fast-moving action, as the camera captures images at 60 fps—but the focus is locked once the first frame is taken. Use Pro Capture Low when the subject is moving erratically, as the camera will continue to focus while shooting—although it captures images at a slower rate of 18 fps. To adjust the Pro Capture settings, go to Menu > Custom Menu > C1 > H Settings (or L Setting), where you can set the Max FPS, Pre-Shutter Frames, and Frame Count Limiter options.

HIGH RES SHOT

Press the Sequential Shooting/Self-Timer/Flash button and rotate the Rear dial to select High Res Shot. Use the Info button to switch between Tripod and Handheld modes, then press OK.

High Res Shot allows you to shoot at a resolution higher than that of the image sensor by taking a series of images and then combining them. It is best used with static subjects due to the sensor moving during capture. Image stabilization cannot be used and anything in motion may be blurred. High Res Shot is available using the P, S, A, and M Shooting modes only.

Go to Menu > Shooting Menu 2 > High Res Shot (icon) to adjust the following options:

High Res Shot: Turn off, or choose how long the camera waits after pressing the Shutter button before a photo is taken.

Flash Charge Time: Choose how long the camera waits for the flash to recharge.

Shooting Method: Options are Tripod and Handheld. If shooting on a tripod, RAW images are captured at 80 megapixels (10368 x 7776), the flash sync speed is 1/50 second, and the maximum ISO is 1600. If shooting handheld, RAW images are captured at 50 megapixels (8160 x 6120), the flash is disabled, and the maximum ISO is 6400.

STARRY SKY AUTOFOCUS

Press the AF/Metering Mode button, then rotate the Rear dial to select [*]AF (Starry Sky AF).

Compose the image and press the AEL/AFL button to initiate starry sky autofocus. The camera displays "[Starry Sky AF is Running]" and the in-focus indicator will be displayed for two seconds once focus is achieved. If focus cannot be achieved, the in-focus indicator will flash. Press the Shutter button all the way down to take the photo.

Note: Use the Menu > Custom Menu > A4 > Starry Sky AF Setting menu to choose between Accuracy (which prioritizes accuracy over speed) and Speed (which prioritizes speed over accuracy).

WIRELESS COMMUNICATION

Pair your camera and smartphone to import and edit photos, use your smartphone as a remote control, and more.

1. Install and launch the OI.Share app on your smartphone.
2. Select Menu > Playback Menu > Wi-Fi Connect and press the Right Arrow key.
3. Select Device Connection and press OK.
4. Press OK after reading the pairing guide.
5. When Connection Setup screen 3 is shown, tap the camera icon at the bottom of the OI.Share app display.
6. Follow the OI.Share app instructions to use a QR code to pair the camera and your smartphone.

RESET CAMERA

Menu > Shooting Menu 1 > Reset/Custom Modes

1. Select Reset, then press the Right Arrow key.
2. Select Basic or Full from the list and press OK. The Basic setting resets basic shooting functions, and the Full setting is a more robust reset (however, it does not reset a number of features, such as Date and Time, Language, Drive mode, Metering mode, and more).
3. Make sure Reset is still selected and press OK.
4. Select Yes on the popup menu and press OK.

05 STEP-BY-STEP SHOOTING INSTRUCTIONS

MULTIPLE EXPOSURES

Create in-camera multiple exposures:

1. Go to Menu > Shooting Menu 2 > Multiple Exposure and press OK.
2. Use the Arrow Key Pad to select from the following:

   Number of Frames: Off turns off multiple exposure shooting, and 2f creates a multiple exposure from two frames.

   Auto Gain: Off or On. On cuts the brightness of each frame in half.

   Overlay: Off means you want to create the multiple exposure from the next two pictures you take. On means you want to shoot a multiple exposure that includes a RAW image that's already on your memory card. If you select On, you'll be prompted to select an image.
3. Press OK, then press Menu.
4. Take photos for the multiple exposure.
5. Press Menu or the Playback button to end multiple exposure shooting.

INTERVAL TIMER SHOOTING / TIME-LAPSE MOVIES

Set the camera to take a series of photos over a period of time or create a time-lapse movie:

1. Go to Menu > Shooting Menu 1 > Intrvl. Sh./Time Lapse, select On, and press the Right Arrow key.
2. Adjust the following settings, then press OK:

   Number of Frames: Number of frames you want to shoot.

   Start Waiting Time: How long before you start shooting.

   Interval Length: How long between each shot.

   Time Lapse Movie: On to create a movie. Off to save individual photos.

   Movie Settings: Choose the frame size and frame rate if you're creating movie.
3. Press OK repeatedly until you're back at Shooting Menu 1.
4. Press Menu to exit the menus.
5. Take photos.

HDR HDR

Combine multiple images to reduce the contrast and improve tonal range:

1. Go to Menu > Shooting Menu 2 > HDR, and press the Right Arrow key.
2. Highlight from the following options, then press OK:

   HDR1 and HDR2: Automatic modes that create a single in-camera HDR image. HDR1 is more natural looking, HDR2 is a more processed and painterly look.

   3f 2.0EV–5f 3.0EV: To bracket a series of exposures so that you can create an HDR image yourself with post-processing software, select one of these five combinations of number of frames along with the amount of exposure change between shots.
3. Press Menu repeatedly until you've exited the menus.
4. Take photos.

06 TYPICAL SHOOTING SCENARIOS

SHOOTING SCENARIO
PORTRAIT

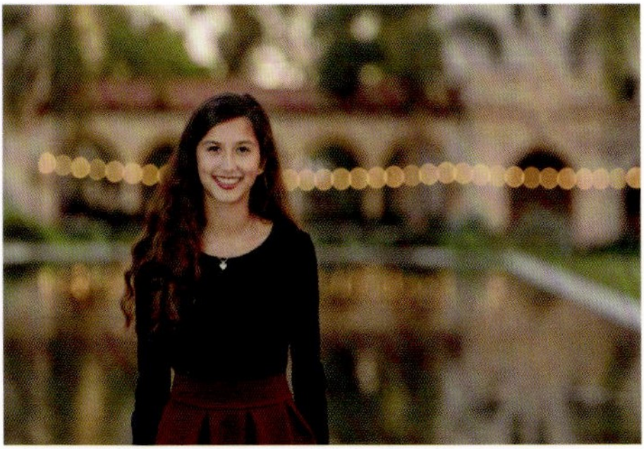

KEY PRINCIPLES

- The key to a portrait like this is shallow depth of field. So shoot in **APERTURE PRIORITY** mode and set the aperture to the lowest aperture your lens offers (such as f/2.8 or f/4).
- Remember to **focus on the eyes**.
- If the image is too dark or too light, use **EXPOSURE COMPENSATION** to adjust the brightness level.

- If the image is blurry from a slow shutter speed, **raise the ISO** to increase your sensor's sensitivity to light, thus allowing for a faster shutter speed.
- Remember to use a **focal length of 50mm or greater** so that you don't distort your subject's face.

SHOOTING SCENARIO
GROUP PORTRAIT

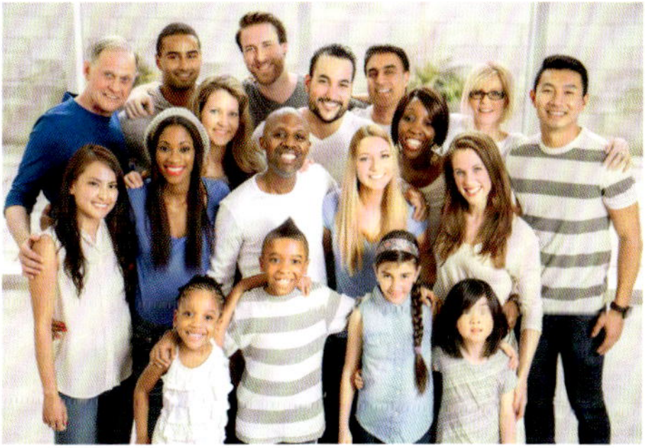

KEY PRINCIPLES

- In order to get everyone in focus, you need a deep depth of field. So shoot in **APERTURE PRIORITY** mode, and set the aperture between **f/8–f/16** for a deeper depth of field.

- **Focus on the person in the middle of the group.** Check focus by zooming in to view it at 100% and check the faces in the group. If anyone is out of focus, use a smaller aperture for deeper depth of field.
- Use **DIGITAL ESP METERING** mode to account for the light in the entire scene.
- **Arrange the group so they can all see you** (and you can see them).
- Use **EXPOSURE COMPENSATION** if the image is too bright or too dark.
- If image is blurry, **raise the ISO** to allow the camera to use a faster shutter speed.

SHOOTING SCENARIO

LANDSCAPE

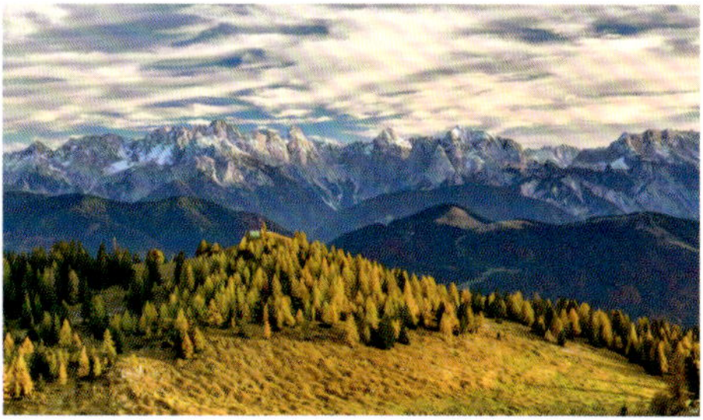

KEY PRINCIPLES

- Shoot in **APERTURE PRIORITY** to control depth of field. Start with **f/16** to ensure deep depth of field.
- **Use a tripod** to eliminate camera movement. Whenever your camera is on a tripod, also make sure **IMAGE STABILIZATION** is turned off.
- Use **DIGITAL ESP METERING** mode and **SINGLE AUTOFOCUS (S-AF)**.
- **Set the ISO to a low setting (L64–200)** to avoid any digital noise.
- Shoot in **RAW** so that you have the most available information when editing later.
- Consider **BRACKETING** your exposures.

SHOOTING SCENARIO

FREEZE ACTION

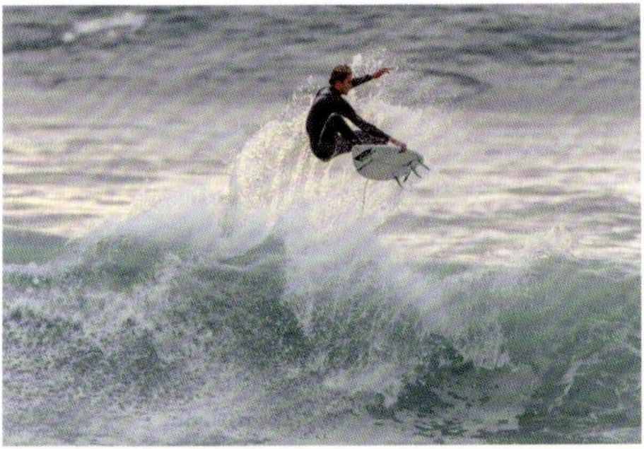

KEY PRINCIPLES

- Use **SHUTTER PRIORITY** mode and set the shutter speed to a value that will freeze the action. The appropriate shutter speed depends on your subject and its movement, but could be anywhere between **1/500–1/8000 sec**.
- Use **CONTINUOUS AUTOFOCUS (C-AF)** so that the camera keeps focusing as the subject moves.
- If the image is dark or blurry, **raise the ISO or try AUTO ISO** to automatically have the camera adjust the ISO as needed.

SHOOTING SCENARIO

SHOWING MOTION—PANNING

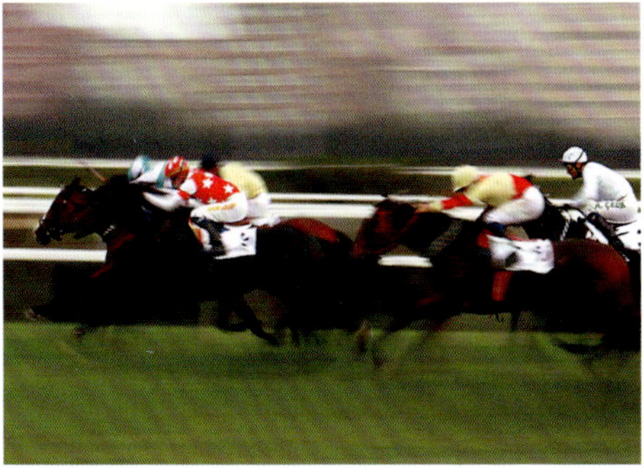

KEY PRINCIPLES

- Shoot in **SHUTTER PRIORITY** mode and set the shutter speed to a value that is slow enough to allow for the subject to move during the exposure.
- **Follow the subject** across the frame as you shoot.
- Try **LIVE VIEW**, which allows you to see the subject during the exposure on the bigger monitor.
- Use **CONTINUOUS AF + TRACKING (C-AF+TR)** so the camera will continue to track the subject as you're panning.

SHOOTING SCENARIO

LOW-LIGHT ACTION

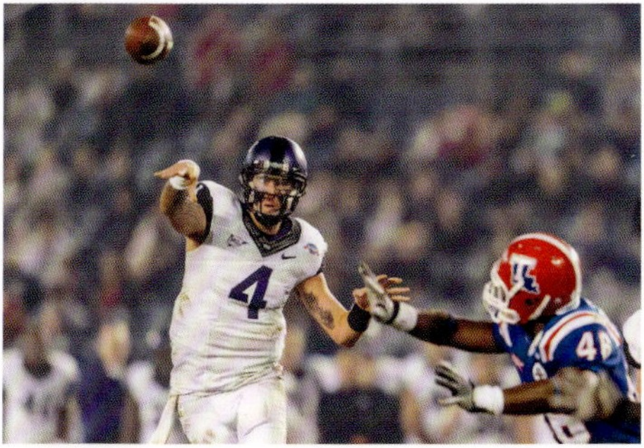

KEY PRINCIPLES

- Shoot in **APERTURE PRIORITY** mode and use a wide aperture such as f/2.8 or f/4.
- Use **SPOT METERING** and meter on the subject's face.
- Use **CONTINUOUS AUTOFOCUS (C-AF)** and a **SINGLE AF TARGET**.
- **Set the ISO to 1600 or higher**, depending on the amount of available light.
- If the image is blurry, **increase the ISO** to allow for a faster shutter speed.

SHOOTING SCENARIO

LONG EXPOSURE

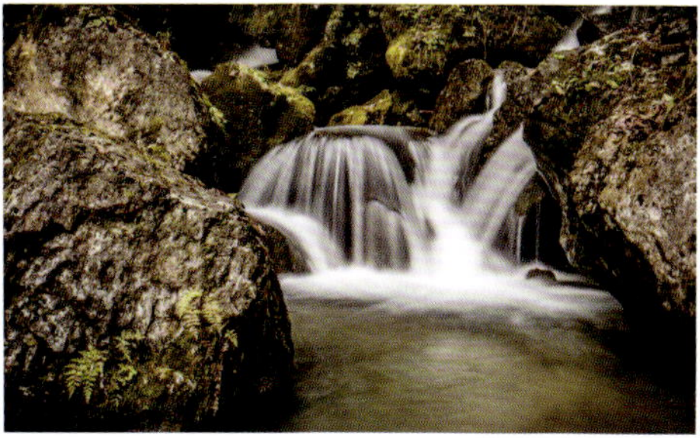

KEY PRINCIPLES

- Shoot either in **BULB** mode, where the shutter stays open as long as the Shutter button is pressed, or **LIVE TIME** mode, where you press the Shutter button once to open the shutter and press it again to end the exposure.
- **Use a tripod** to keep the camera stable. **Turn off IMAGE STABILIZATION**.
- Use the **SINGLE AUTOFOCUS (S-AF)** mode, or try **manual focus** if the camera is having a hard time locking on focus.
- **Use a low ISO (L64–400)** and shoot **RAW** to ensure a high-quality file.
- For night sky photos, try the **[*] STARRY SKY AUTOFOCUS** mode.

SHOOTING SCENARIO

MACRO/CLOSE-UP

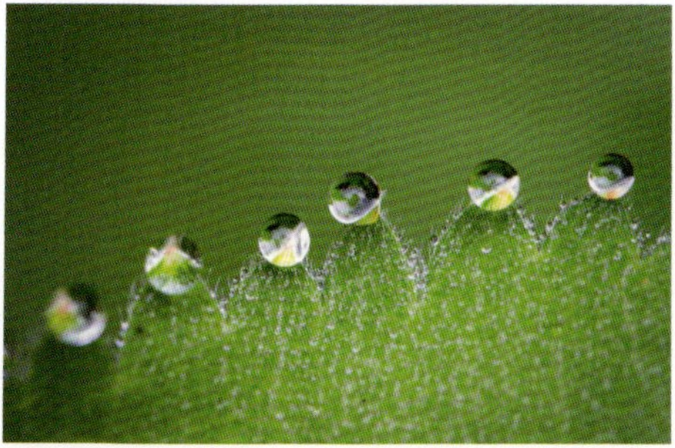

KEY PRINCIPLES

- Shoot in **APERTURE PRIORITY** mode and **use a small aperture** to ensure you achieve enough depth of field (this image was shot at f/13).
- Use **DIGITAL ESP METERING** to analyze the light in the entire frame.
- A **tripod** is very useful for keeping the camera steady.
- Use **MANUAL FOCUS** and **zoom in** to confirm your focus is tack-sharp.
- Try using a dedicated **macro lens or close-up filters** to make sure you can achieve sharp focus when you're so close to the subject.